NATURE'S MYSTERIES

HOW MONKEYS "TALK"

Martin Banks

BENCHMARK BOOKS

MARSHALL CAVENDISH
NEW YORK

Benchmark Books
Marshall Cavendish Corporation
99 White Plains Road
Tarrytown, New York 10591-9001

©Marshall Cavendish Corporation, 1999

Series created by Discovery Books

Library of Congress Cataloging-in-Publication Data
Banks, Martin, 1947-
    How Monkeys "Talk"/Martin Banks
    p. cm. - (Nature's Mysteries)
    Includes bibliographical references (p.) and index.
    Summary: Explains how monkeys and other primates communicate, by means of facial expressions,
    vocal sounds, scents, and body language.
    ISBN 0-7614-0858-4
    1. Primates - Behavior - Juvenile literature. 2. Animal communication - Juvenile literature. 3. Monkeys
    - behavior - Juvenile literature. [1. Primates. 2. Animal communication. 3. Monkeys.]
    I. Title. II. Series
    QL737.P9B265 1998   98-20530   CIP AC
    599.8'159 - DC21

Printed in Hong Kong

Acknowledgments
Text consultant: Professor J. Patrick Gray, Department of Anthropology, University of Wisconsin, Milwaukee.
Illustrated by Robert Morton.
The publishers would like to thank the following for their permission to reproduce photographs: cover Tero
Niemi/Bruce Coleman, title page Erwin & Peggy Bauer/Bruce Coleman, 4 bottom David Hosking/FLPA, 4 top
K.G. Preston-Mafham/Premaphotos Wildlife, 5 Lawrence Migdale/Photo Researchers/Oxford Scientific Films, 6
bottom Erwin & Peggy Bauer/ Bruce Coleman, 6 top Rod Williams/Bruce Coleman. 7 Jim Tuten/Animals
Animals/Oxford Scientific Films, 8 Panda/E. Coppola/FLPA, 9 top Konrad Wothe/Bruce Coleman, 9 bottom Frank
Lane/FLPA, 10 Winfried Wisniewski/FLPA, 11 top Johnny Johnson/Bruce Coleman, 11 bottom Silvestris/FLPA, 12
E. & D. Hosking/FLPA, 13 Alain Compost/Bruce Coleman, 14 Gunter Ziesler/Bruce Coleman, 15 top Peter
Davey/FLPA, 17 K.G. Preston-Mafham/Premaphotos Wildlife, 18 Silvestris/FLPA, 19 Michael Leach/Oxford
Scientific Films, 20 Christer Fredriksson/Bruce Coleman, 21 K.G. Preston-Mafham/Premaphotos Wildlife, 22
bottom R.I.M. Campbell/Bruce Coleman, 22 top K.G. Preston-Mafham/Premaphotos Wildlife, 24 bottom Erwin
and Peggy Bauer/Bruce Coleman, 24 top Mark Newman/FLPA, 25 Jim Clare/Oxford Scientific Films, 26 Rod
Williams/Bruce Coleman, 27 Winfried Wisniewski/FLPA, 28 Frank Lane/FLPA, 29 Barry Britton/BBC Natural
History Unit.

(Cover) A green monkey howling, Masai Mara, Kenya.

CONTENTS

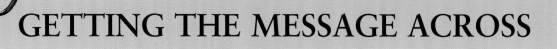
Have you ever thought about how you communicate with other people? You use language, of course, but there are many other ways of giving signals and letting others know what is going on. The expression on your face and the way you move can tell people a lot.

Animals don't use speech as we do, but they have many fascinating ways of communicating with each other. Monkeys and apes in particular have the ability to share information and feelings by using sounds, scents, and movements.

Monkeys and apes, as well as humans, belong to a large and varied group of animals called primates. Primates can be divided into two main groups: the prosimians and the anthropoids. Prosimians are the more primitive animals, such as lemurs, lorises, and bush babies. Some of them, the dwarf lemur for instance, are barely larger than a mouse.

◀▲ *Monkeys live almost entirely in the tropical regions of the world, including Africa, South and Central America, and Southeast Asia. Many species, like the gray langurs from India (above), spend their whole lives high in the tree canopy of tropical rain forests. Others live on the forest floor or, like these African baboons (left), on the open grasslands.*

Monkeys, apes, and humans are the anthropoids, or higher primates. They range from the tiniest marmoset to the largest gorilla. Monkeys and apes have much in common with humans: their expressive faces have forward-looking eyes and mobile lips, and their hands can perform intricate tasks. Their societies also have similarities to our own.

Most species live in highly organized groups, and clear communication is vital to their existence. We're going to look at how monkeys and their fellow primates can "talk" to each other.

The facial expressions of a chimpanzee can show alarm, pleasure, and anger. Other chimpanzees know exactly what the message is.

MONKEY VOICES

In a Colombian rain forest, a large troop of black-capped Capuchin monkeys are feeding in the trees. As they move through the branches, each monkey gives a series of soft, low whistles to its neighbors. They use a louder and higher-pitched call to the more distant members of the group. These contact calls help keep the monkeys together as they travel through the forest.

▼ *Capuchins spend most of their lives in the top canopy of the trees. Arboreal monkeys such as these use their calls to keep track of group members. This helps them stay together and also stops them from bumping into other groups in the thick foliage.*

▲ *Many monkeys have loud voices that they use to good effect. Some even have built-in amplifiers to make their calls louder. Howler monkeys have hollow air sacs and a special bone in their throats to help magnify their roaring calls.*

On the whole, the noisiest monkeys are those, like the Capuchins, that live high in the trees. Because they can't always see each other, their sounds are important for keeping in touch.

Besides contact calls, monkeys have many other vocal expressions. Special sounds and calls pass on messages or show feelings. Baboons live mostly on the ground, where it is easy to keep an eye on the rest of the group. They use sounds for more specific messages, such as warnings or threats.

Among the apes, chimpanzees are well known for chattering and screaming. They often show their excitement with loud hooting calls. If a chimpanzee suddenly discovers a source of abundant fruit, its loud hoots quickly summon the other chimpanzees in the group.

Not all primates have loud voices. The squirrel-sized marmosets and tamarins of South America have high-pitched twittering calls. They sound more like birds than monkeys!

Adult male orangutans warn off rivals by giving a series of long, bubbling notes produced by their large throat sacs. These notes, known as long calls, can be heard more than a half a mile (one kilometer) away.

7

STAKING A CLAIM

Monkeys and other primates are especially vocal when they want to advertise their presence to others. Their loud voices act as a warning to neighboring groups not to trespass into a particular area.

Guenon monkeys live high up in the canopy of the African rain forests. Here the stillness is often broken by a sudden chorus of deep, booming calls. This is the sound of adult male guenons claiming their territories.

Spider monkeys in South America have a short bark for the same purpose, while langurs in Asia let out a whoop.

Territorial calls begin early in the morning. As soon as they wake up, adult male howlers roar loud challenges to each other. They will roar again when they move to a new feeding place, or if they meet another group.

The adult males in a group of monkeys usually chooses a high vantage point in the trees, from which to give the loud calls which will warn other groups of their presence. Macaques live in large groups in the forests of Asia.

◄ When an Indris lemur starts its morning call, other Indris soon begin to join in. This allows each group to know how far away its neighbors are before they begin feeding.

▼ Gibbons live in small family units of a male, a female, and one or two of their youngest offspring. The adult pair establishes a territory with their distinctive combined calls.

Lemurs in Madagascar start early, too. Every morning, their chorus of earsplitting shrieks and wails rings through the forest.

Gibbons, the smallest of the apes, are found in the forests of Southeast Asia. Each pair of gibbons lives together for many years. Over time they develop a duet, a complicated system of bubbling noises that blend with each other, showing that a mated pair of gibbons is in possession of a territory.

SOUNDING THE ALARM

A troop of African baboons is feeding in the grassland. While most of them are busy searching the ground for seeds and insects, one or two act as sentries, keeping a lookout for predators. Suddenly, one sees a suspicious movement in the grass. It stares fixedly at the spot and gives a series of sharp, dog-like barks. Other baboons look nervously around and bark their own alarm calls before fleeing into the safety of the trees.

Baboons and impalas often feed side by side during the day. With their keen hearing and sense of smell, the impalas are the first to notice a predator hiding in the bush. But, in the open grassland, all the animals rely on the baboons' sharp eyes. The two species recognize each other's alarm calls, and they all will respond.

Some species of monkey, like the vervet, have a variety of alarm calls, one for each enemy. The vervet uses different calls for snakes, eagles, and leopards. One call, used only for eagles, will cause the monkeys to look up at the sky before they rush for cover. The alarm for snakes will cause a different reaction, and the monkeys will search the ground for danger.

◀▲ *Vervet monkeys roam the African grasslands in groups, but dash for safety from the ground to the trees when they hear the leopard alarm.*

The alarm calls that monkeys use also help other animals. Their keen eyesight and vantage points up in the trees mean that monkeys are often the first to spot danger below. When a troop of Indian langurs see a tiger on the prowl, they start to give sharp coughs of alarm. Deer and other inhabitants of the forest also become alert when they hear the langurs call, for they understand the message, too.

WHO'S IN CHARGE?

Monkeys, apes, and other primates have ways of communicating that are just as important as their vocal messages. One of the simplest is body language, where an animal shows how it feels by its posture and movements.

In many primate societies, body language is used to show which animal is the dominant member of its group. Using posture and gestures to assert authority is important: it prevents unnecessary fighting and keeps the group in order.

A physical clue to the seniority of a male gorilla is the patch of silver hair on its back. The dominant male in any group of gorillas is always a silverback. Male gorillas also have a special stiff-legged walk called strutting, which shows off their large, powerful bodies to good effect.

The rhesus macaque monkey with his tail curled above his back is obviously the leader of the group. The posture of the subordinate male shows that he knows his place in the order of things and doesn't want to be noticed.

The males in the macaque family of monkeys have a distinct way of showing their rank. A dominant rhesus macaque walks with his rump held high and tail curled above his back. Lower-ranking macaques walk with their backs held low and their tails trailing down. If a male moves up the social ladder, his attitude and body posture will quickly change too.

Apes also show their superiority by body language. A male orangutan will simply stand on all fours in a very obvious position on a branch. This is an easy and effective way to demonstrate its huge size and power, to males and females alike.

▶ *Adult male orangutans are more than twice the size of the females and are immensely powerful.*

VENTING FEELINGS

Primates are unique among animals in the way they express their feelings. Scientists believe that apes have emotions similar to humans: they express excitement, curiosity, unease, and affection. They show how they are feeling in both obvious and subtle ways.

A meeting between two adult male gorillas gives rise to some puzzling behavior. One will suddenly rise to its feet, beat its chest rapidly with its hands to produce a hollow sound, and then drop on all fours again. It may then throw a broken branch in the air.

The gorilla is showing that it is upset by the presence of a rival. While it decides whether to attack or flee, it relieves its confused feelings with some apparently unrelated behavior. This is called displacement activity.

When a male baboon is uncertain it may give a wide yawn. This also exposes its large canine teeth, which may advertise its strength to rival males.

Gorillas are also known to start eating when they are nervous, just as some humans bite their nails or eat when they are nervous.

Hooting   *Symbolic feeding*   *Standing erect*   *Hurling vegetation*

When excited, chimpanzees often pound on the forest trees, creating a booming noise like a drum. Shaking branches and stamping are other favorite distractions. A male baboon, uncertain whether to attack or flee from a rival male, may sit down and open its mouth in a yawn. It is not tired or bored, however. This is another displacement activity, a way of dealing with indecision.

▶ *Chimpanzees often climb high into the trees when excited. They may also leap about, breaking off branches and leaves and hurling them into the air or down onto the ground.*

▼ *Gorillas use a special display when they are excited or upset, as a way of relieving tension. The display is actually a series of separate actions that usually occur in a set order. Often they happen so quickly that they seem to be a single activity lasting just a few seconds.*

Chest beating and leg kicking   *Running sideways*   *Uprooting vegetation*   *Ground thumping*

MAKING FACES

We've already learned that the forward-looking faces and mobile features of the higher primates are very expressive. Some of their facial expressions are remarkably similar to our own, but they don't always mirror the same feelings.

Like humans, monkeys can communicate fear, surprise, playfulness, or uncertainty through their facial expressions. This is very useful in what are generally sociable animals. It's especially necessary for one primate to recognize anger in

Chimpanzees have the most expressive faces of all primates. Their mobile lips allow them to use a wide variety of expressions to show their feelings. Because chimpanzees are the primates most closely related to humans many of their expressions are similar to our own.

Attention

Anxiety

Fear

Aggression

Play

16

another. A direct stare is one of the most important primate signals. It is always a sign of hostility or anger.

Monkeys have other ways of showing their hostility to each other. An open mouth may show that the monkey is thinking of biting. The threat is perfectly clear, and the animal doesn't actually have to bite to get its message across.

Black-and-white colobus monkeys have a different version of this behavior. When they are angry, they smack their lips noisily by opening their mouths sharply, as if surprised. But when two rival langurs meet, they stare fiercely at each other and then grind their teeth noisily as a warning. This may help prevent a fight.

Teeth grinding is used by male gray langurs as a form of warning or threat to a rival male. At the same time, each male displays its sharp, canine teeth. This is often sufficient to prevent them from actually fighting.

17

KEEPING THE PEACE

Monkeys can use their faces and body language to send out friendly messages as well as threatening ones.

The expressions they make with their lips and eyes can prevent attack by another, more aggressive member of the group. This is called appeasement. Body language can appease, too. When monkeys are in trouble with a superior, many species will present their hindquarters to admit their inferior status. The message is, "I give in."

Many primates use grooming to maintain friendly relations in the group. The practical purpose of grooming is to pick dirt and parasites out of each other's fur, but its social function is just as important.

Monkeys and apes use gestures to invite others to approach them. Opening and closing the mouth while smacking the lips rapidly together means in monkey language, "I don't mean any harm" or "Come and join me."

Marmosets, baboons, and mandrills use an expression to show their friendliness that, to us, may look like an aggressive signal. They draw back their lips to expose bared teeth, and at the same time shake their heads from side to side. An extension of this is an expression, known as a playface, that is found in many of the higher primates. Chimpanzees draw back their lips to show their lower teeth and gums and make a chuckling noise that resembles human laughter. Similar to a human smile, this expression is clearly an invitation to play.

The open-mouth expression of a chimpanzee shows that it is in a relaxed or playful mood.

Some monkeys have brightly colored faces and almost equally colorful hindquarters. These play an important function in helping them keep in contact with each other.

With its scarlet and blue-ridged face, the adult male mandrill is among the most colorful of all mammals. This bizarre color scheme is repeated in luminous colors on the tail and rear. Mandrills live deep in the rain forest where little sunlight penetrates to the forest floor. The male mandrill's face and rear show up in the dark and help other members of the troop keep track of their leaders.

Other monkeys also use color signals as a way of identifying

The male mandrill's colorful face serves as a badge of its high rank, but it also helps other members of its group see it in the dark forest.

their own species. This is very important to guenons, because several different kinds may live in one patch of forest. Each species of guenon has its own distinctive pattern of markings on the face and body that can be used like identification badges.

The ring-tailed lemur has a long, bushy tail marked with distinctive rings of black and white. As they move along, these lemurs wave their tails in the air like flags in a kind of follow-the-leader activity to help the whole group stay together.

Ring-tailed lemurs are unusual among lemurs in that they spend part of their day on the ground. Their long tails act as a signaling device to others in the group as they move between the trees.

WHAT'S THAT SMELL?

If you walk through a forest and look upward, the forest canopy may look like a tangled maze. But to the monkeys and other primates that live in it, the branches of the trees provide a series of regular routes along which they travel from one part of the forest to another. These aerial pathways have the same purpose as our own roads and footpaths down on the ground. Many primates use scents to mark their paths through the treetops.

The prosimian primates include such species as slow lorises, bush babies, and tarsiers. These small, simple creatures are usually only active at night, so visual signals aren't very useful to them in communicating with each other. Many prosimians are solitary, which means that the sounds used

▲ *Lemurs travel chiefly in the trees. Scent-marking the branches helps the members of a lemur troop keep in contact with each other.*

by primates that live in groups are not very helpful either. Instead, these animals use their scents to communicate with each other.

Prosimians may have poorer vision than monkeys and apes, but they have a far superior sense of smell. They also have special scent-producing glands on their bodies. As they travel through the trees, they rub these glands onto the branches. The smell they produce leaves a scent message for others of the same species to read when they pass the same way.

◄ *Some nocturnal primates, such as these bush babies, have little use for the keen eyesight found in higher primates. They rely much more on their sense of smell.*

Stink-fighting by ring-tailed lemurs prevents any real fight from taking place.

Ring-tailed lemurs have scent glands situated in their armpits and on their forearms. They wipe scent from these glands onto their long tails and then hold them aloft. The scent wafts toward members of a rival group to warn them away. This is known as stink-fighting, and it usually results in the retreat of one group or the other.

The little South American squirrel monkeys use scent to mark their territories. They urinate on their hands and feet, and then smear branches with their smell as they move along specific pathways through the trees. This smell firmly announces their territorial boundaries, but it also may leave a trail for others in the group to follow.

FINDING A MATE

For primates, finding a mate is as important as it is for all animals. Monkeys and apes can use their voices and body language in their search for a partner. In primate society, it is often only the biggest and strongest male that mates with the females. He needs to be clearly recognizable to all, and this is achieved by a combination of size and calls that only develop when the males are fully grown.

▼ *Mangabey monkeys have distinctive white flashes on their eyelids that can be seen from a great distance. It is thought that mangabeys use their eyelids to communicate with each other. But it is the whoop-gobble of the mature male that attracts female mangabeys.*

▲ *When it is mature, a male orangutan develops wide pads of fat on his cheeks that help identify him as a worthy mate.*

Mangabey monkeys inhabit the forests of Central Africa. The adult males have a call known as a whoop-gobble, which serves as a territorial signal. The females recognize that any male using this call is a fully grown adult, and they are attracted to him as a partner rather than to younger males in the group.

Adult male orangutans do not live in a group. They establish their own large territories, which may be inhabited by several females. Fully grown males use their far-carrying long calls to warn off other males and to attract females.

The white-faced saki monkeys of South America and several species of gibbons live in pairs, accompanied by their offspring. When they reach adolescence, the young animals have to leave the family group and look for their own mate. In both these species, the two sexes are differently colored, which helps males and females identify each other when they are looking for partners.

In a few species of primates, like these saki monkeys, males and females are colored differently. This is known as sexual diamorphism.

LEARNING THE LANGUAGE

How do young monkeys manage to learn all the calls, facial expressions, and body language that will be so important in their future lives?

Primates learn mostly from observing and copying what others in the group do, particularly their mothers. A baby monkey remains with its mother for two years or more. Young apes are not fully independent until the age of five or six, or even older in the case of the orangutan. During this period of growing up, they acquire all the signs and signals of their species that are necessary for adult life.

Young chimpanzees stay close to their mothers at all times. By watching and imitating her gestures and expressions, they prepare themselves for adulthood and independence.

Young primates need to learn which messages are used in which situations. When a group of gorillas has spread out to feed in tall vegetation, they keep in contact with each other by using a series of rumbling sounds that resemble belching. A young gorilla learns to distinguish between this peaceful sound and alarm noises, like screams and sharp barks.

In the simplest prosimians, the learning period lasts only a few months, but the slow-growing apes

Playing with other youngsters in the group is essential to monkeys and apes. They practice the body language and social skills needed to get along with the group.

take several years to learn the full range of signals and messages. Monkeys and apes raised in experiments by humans are often unable to mix normally with their own kind when they grow up. Learning social and communication skills is something they must do among their own species and while they are young.

There is no doubt that monkeys and apes are among the most advanced communicators in the animal kingdom. Chimpanzees, gorillas, and baboons in particular have a wide range of calls and expressions. Some people think these forms of communication should be regarded as a language.

In recent years a theory has been developed that apes can be taught to understand human language. Scientists have tried to teach chimpanzees to say words, but they have had little success. The animals just don't have the right vocal chords and mouth structure for producing speech.

Chimpanzees will respond to facial expressions made by humans, but it is unlikely that they can actually be taught to talk a human language.

In the United States during the 1960s, a chimpanzee called Washoe was taught to use sign language. The fact that she was able to put together verbs, nouns, and other words to make her own sentences led some people to believe she could apply the principles of language. However, other scientists doubted that Washoe really understood the signs she was making. They said she was simply imitating what she had been taught.

Other chimpanzees and gorillas have taken part in experiments to see if they can understand human language by using a bank of computerized symbols that they touch to make words. Some apes seem to have mastered this method to make simple sentences. But so far, none of these clever apes has learned to talk, and the debate continues.

A chimpanzee painting. Some scientists think that primate paintings may give us some clues to the origins of human art.

GLOSSARY

appeasement: the act of pacifying or trying to please in order to avoid a conflict.

arboreal: living in trees.

canopy: the thick network of branches and leaves in the treetops, which in a forest often completely blocks out the light.

communication: a way of passing on or exchanging information.

dominant: an animal that has a higher rank than others in its group.

hostility: a feeling or action of unfriendliness.

primate: all members of the order of primates, which includes apes, monkeys, prosimians, and humans.

prosimian: a suborder of primates, which includes the simple, less advanced species such as lorises and lemurs.

subordinate: an animal which has a lower rank than others in its group.

territory: the area within which an animal has its home and which it defends against others of the same species.

FURTHER READING

Ashby, Ruth. *The Orangutan*. Minneapolis: Dillon Press, 1994.

Freedman, Suzanne. *Dian Fossey: Befriending the Gorillas*. Austin: Raintree/Steck-Vaughn, 1997.

Gelmanish, Rita Golden. *Monkeys and Apes of the World*. New York: Franklin Watts, 1990.

Grace, Eric. *Apes*. San Francisco: Sierra Club Wildlife Library, 1995.

Harman, Amanda and Rudolf Steiner. *South American Monkeys*. New York: Marshall Cavendish Corporation, 1996.

Miller-Schroeder, Patricia and Karen Dudley. *Gorillas*. Austin: Raintree/Steck Vaughn, 1997.

Redmond, Ian, et al. *Gorilla*. New York: Knopf, 1995.

Tattersall, Ian. *Primates: Lemurs, Monkeys, and You*. Brookfield: Millbrook Press, 1995.

INDEX

Numbers in *italic* indicate pictures